THE
ABUNDANCE
BOOK

OTHER HAY HOUSE PRODUCTS
BY JOHN RANDOLPH PRICE

Books

The Abundance Book (pocket-sized tradepaper edition)
The Alchemist's Handbook
Empowerment
The Jesus Code
The Love Book
The Meditation Book
Nothing Is Too Good to Be True
Practical Spirituality
Removing the Masks That Bind Us
A Spiritual Philosophy for the New World
The Success Book
The Wellness Book
With Wings As Eagles
The Workbook for Self-Mastery

Audio/CD

The 40-Day Prosperity Plan

All of the above are available at
your local bookstore, or may be ordered by visiting:
Hay House USA: **www.hayhouse.com**
Hay House Australia: **www.hayhouse.com.au**
Hay House UK: **www.hayhouse.co.uk**
Hay House South Africa: **orders@psdprom.co.za**

THE ABUNDANCE BOOK

John Randolph Price

HAY HOUSE, INC.
Carlsbad, California
London • Sydney • Johannesburg
Vancouver • Hong Kong

Published and distributed in the United States by: Hay House, Inc., P.O. Box 5100, Carlsbad, CA 92018-5100 • *Phone:* (760) 431-7695 or (800) 654-5126 • *Fax:* (760) 431-6948 or (800) 650-5115 • www.hayhouse.com • **Published and distributed in Australia by:** Hay House Australia Pty. Ltd., 18/36 Ralph St., Alexandria NSW 2015 • *Phone:* 612-9669-4299 • *Fax:* 612-9669-4144 • www.hayhouse.com.au • **Published and distributed in the United Kingdom by:** Hay House UK, Ltd. • Unit 62, Canalot Studios • 222 Kensal Rd., London W10 5BN • *Phone:* 44-20-8962-1230 • *Fax:* 44-20-8962-1239 • www.hayhouse.co.uk • **Published and distributed in the Republic of South Africa by:** Hay House SA (Pty.), Ltd., P.O. Box 990, Witkoppen 2068 • *Phone/Fax:* 2711-7012233 • orders@psdprom.co.za • **Distributed in Canada by:** Raincoast • 9050 Shaughnessy St., Vancouver, B.C. V6P 6E5 • *Phone:* (604) 323-7100 • *Fax:* (604) 323-2600

Editorial supervision: Jill Kramer   *Design:* Amy Gingery

Library of Congress Cataloging-in-Publication Data

Price, John Randolph.
    The abundance book / John Randolph Price.
        p. cm.
    ISBN 1-4019-0475-0 (hardcover)
    1. Finance, Personal—Religious aspects. 2. New Thought. I. Title.
    HG179.P7357 2005
    332.024—dc22

                                                    2004001044

                            ISBN 1-4019-0475-0

                    07   06   05   04   4 3 2 1
                1st hardcover printing, December 2004

                Printed in the United States of America

CONTENTS

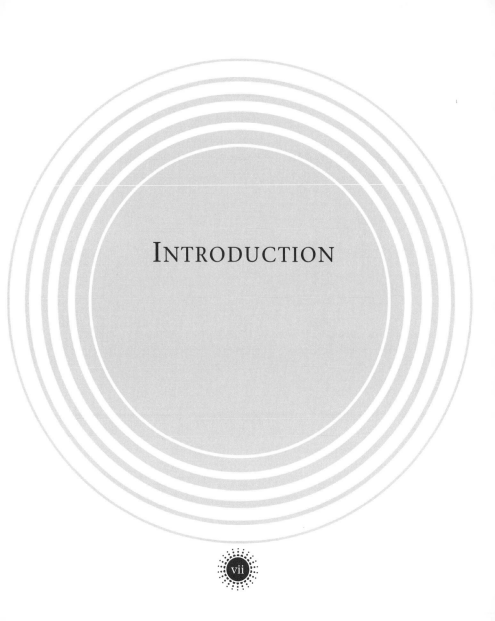

INTRODUCTION

S ince the beginning of the civilized world, enlightened ones have taught that prosperity is a part of the natural process of life, and that lavish abundance is the unquestionable nature of each individual. And through the centuries, countless men and women accepted this truth, realized the law of infinite plenty within, and moved above the illusion of scarcity into the reality of unlimited wealth. They proved for themselves that the energy of abundance is constantly radiating from the Source within and flowing out to appear as money and financial well-being.

What one has done, all can do. The secret is to be aware of this unfailing principle, to understand that lack is simply the outpicturing of false beliefs, and to know that as you make the correction in consciousness, you will become a channel for the activity of ever-expanding affluence in your life.

The purpose of this book is to provide you with an easy-to-read collection of prosperity ideas for quick study and reference. You can refer to it throughout the day to remind you that you are the wealth of the Universe individualized—and that the only limitations you have are the ones you've imposed upon yourself. In Part I, the message of prosperity is traced through the ages; in Part II, you'll find The 40-Day Prosperity Plan from my book *The Workbook for Self-Mastery,* as well as an introduction to the enclosed CD. Part III was written to help you condition your consciousness for a deeper understanding of the energy of money, and Part IV is a prosperity compilation from some of my other books.

This material certainly isn't the last word on the subject of supply. However, if you practice the principles and dedicate yourself to opening consciousness to the infinite riches within, it won't be long before you awaken to your Divine inheritance. And with each awakening, more of the error patterns of lack and limitation are erased from the collective consciousness. The good of the whole *does* begin with each individual.

— **John Randolph Price**

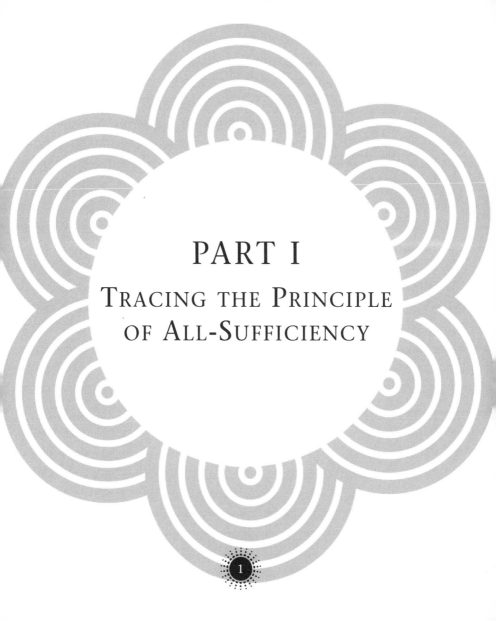

PART I

TRACING THE PRINCIPLE OF ALL-SUFFICIENCY

This book couldn't possibly cover all the teachings on abundance that have flowed through the channels of Ageless Wisdom—and which have then been adapted by Western culture and reinterpreted as spiritual metaphysics. The concept of *all-sufficiency* was a building block of essentially all philosophical and religious systems (in their original form) until the second-century A.D., when the war against self-knowledge and self-reliance began.

The Ancients taught that to understand oneself was to understand God, and through the process of meditation, one could release the Divine energy from within and transmute discord into harmony, ignorance into wisdom, fear into love, and lack into abundance. The initiate was trained to conceive the highest and noblest ideas as the vision for manifestation, and then to identify the symbols of the vision with the Master Spirit within—the Source of all.

Students of the Mysteries were also instructed in the use of the innate radiatory and magnetic powers in exercising dominion. By working with the rhythmic Energy of Self, whatever form that was needed for exchange (the legal tender of that time) was brought forth as an instrument of *goodwill.* As such, "money" was simply a token of appreciation of one's service, a symbol of love and integrity.

Regardless of the level of instruction, one particular teaching remained constant throughout the initiation process: Mind and emotions embodying love, gentleness, and peace eliminated limitation— that is, such a consciousness of *harmlessness* freed an individual from the bonds and restrictions of human thought.

The Mystery Schools of Asia, Egypt, Persia, and Greece provided an invaluable service to humankind by reawakening the spiritual powers in a core group of dedicated men and women. This knowledge of harmony and fulfillment continued in sacred books and secret teachings—in the Hebrew Kabbalah, in the beliefs of Hindu and Buddhist mystics, in the Gnostic writings of early Christianity, and in certain passages not removed from the Bible.

Through the inspiration and teachings of Jesus, the Gnostics (from the Greek word *gnosis,* which means "knowledge") continued the esoteric tradition. Their writings emphasized the Oneness of God and man, the divinity of the individual, and the creative power of each soul to rise above limitation. In the Nag Hammadi texts discovered in Egypt in 1945—considered older than the New Testament gospels—we have a literal library of gnostic writings. In the *Gospel of Thomas,* one of 52 books found, Jesus makes it clear that when you know your true identity, you'll realize that you're one with the Living

Father. And then to emphasize the Truth that your consciousness of the Presence within constitutes your supply, Jesus says: "But if you will not know yourselves, then you dwell in poverty, and it is you who are that poverty."

From the *Gospel of Philip,* we're reminded of the esoteric practice of transforming vision into manifest form: " . . . what you see you shall become." The Gnostics worshiped the pure spiritual Light of the indwelling Christ, and through their knowledge of thought-form energy and the principles of manifestation, they were able to cooperate with Spirit in the releasing of the creative powers—at least for nearly 300 years following Jesus' time on Earth.

In A.D. 180, Irenaeus, the bishop of Lyons, attacked independent thinking and all teachings relating to the Oneness of God and individual man/woman. Believing that a spiritual consciousness and a personal union with God would undermine the authority of the priests, he directed his wrath upon Gnosticism. First he issued his five-volume

Against Heresies, followed by a list of acceptable writings—choosing only those words that supported his demand for a fixed dogma. The shift in mind-direction from within to without had begun, and the innate power of the individual was gradually given to an outer structure and a lower authority.

When emperor Theodosius made Christianity the sole and official religion of the state in A.D. 380, the Institution assumed complete control over individual minds, and humanity entered the thousand-year period referred to as the Dark Ages. In fact, the first 400 years of this period is considered the "barren age" in Europe, as few advances in literature, science, and education were contributed to the future of the human race.

During that time, what is known today as a "prosperity consciousness"—the realization of God as the Source of all good—was almost nonexistent. The feudal system controlled secular life, and the keys to spiritual enlightenment were held by the Church leaders. Too free a subjective interpretation of the doctrine or lack of faith in the state religion resulted in extreme penalties. Due to the constant struggle between the Church and the individual, the mastery techniques dealing with freedom from need and the science of forces and forms were temporarily lost. The Western mind was kept "in the dark" until the institutional structure began to crack in the 1500s, and the eternal principles of Oneness and Unity began to resurface.

The Rosicrucians, also called "The Fraternity of the Rosy Cross," began to exert influence to counteract religious intolerance, remaining essentially underground until the publication of the Order's manifesto in 1614. Following the traditions of the ancient Egyptians and the Christian Gnostics, members of the secret society were known to transcend the limitations of the physical world through their spiritual awakening—overcoming lack through Knowledge (realization) of the Presence and Will of God.

Freemasonry—"more ancient than any of the world's living religions," according to Albert Pike—

continued the chain of the sacred Mysteries. Through an understanding of spiritual Reality and a dedication to Wisdom, Love, and Service, the Master Masons attained "supernatural" powers, with the ability to bring an all-sufficiency of visible supply out of the invisible substance. The (human) race mind was beginning to feel the effect of this new Light of Understanding.

By the 1800s, esoteric philosophy and practical mysticism were moving across Europe and America like a tidal wave. The Transcendental Movement led by Ralph Waldo Emerson began in New England; the Metaphysical Movement was ushered in by Phineas Quimby; Helena P. Blavatsky and Henry Olcott founded the Theosophical Society; Mary Baker Eddy founded Christian Science; the New Thought Movement blossomed through the work and teachings of Charles and Myrtle Fillmore (Unity), Nona Brooks (Divine Science), and Ernest Holmes (Religious Science); Alice Bailey established the Arcane School; Rudolf Steiner formed the

Anthroposophical Society; Paramahansa Yogananda founded the Self-Realization Fellowship; and out of the wealth of material in the Edgar Cayce files grew the Association for Research and Enlightenment— to name but a few contributors to the New Age of spiritual unfoldment.

It's now estimated that at least 25 percent of the population of America is involved in some measure with what is considered Esoteric Philosophy or New Thought Religion. And right in the mainstream of this consciousness is the Truth that God is boundless wealth, and as expressions of the Infinite, we have an abundant inheritance.

This Message of Prosperity couldn't be concealed—not even in the Bible. With more than 2,000 years of censoring, editing, and translating, the Golden Light of the Father's Assurance remains. For example:

"Beloved, I wish above all things that thou mayest prosper . . . " (3 John 1:2)

"'Prove me now herewith,' said the Lord of hosts, 'if I will not open you the windows of heaven and pour you out a blessing that there shall not be room enough to receive it.'" (Malachi 3:10)

"The blessing of the Lord, it maketh rich, and He addeth no sorrow with it." (Proverbs 10:22)

"They shall prosper that love Thee. Peace be within thy walls, and prosperity within thy palaces." (Psalm 122:6–7)

"God is able to make all grace abound toward you; that ye, always having all-sufficiency in all things may abound to every good work." (2 Corinthians 9:8)

"Thou shalt remember the Lord thy God, for it is he that giveth thee power to get wealth . . . " (Deuteronomy 8:18)

"The Lord shall open unto thee his good treasure, the heaven to give the rain unto thy land in his season, and to bless all the work of thine hand; and thou shalt lend unto many nations, and thou shalt not borrow." (Deuteronomy 28:12)

"Let the Lord be magnified which hath pleasure in the prosperity of his servant." (Psalm 35:27)

"All things whatsoever ye pray and ask for, believe that ye have received them and ye shall have them." (Mark 11:12)

And the Message continues:

"Man was born to be rich, or grows rich by the use of his faculties, by the union of thought with nature." — Ralph Waldo Emerson

"The world, with all its beauty, its happiness and suffering, its joys and pains, is planned with

the utmost ingenuity, in order that the powers of the Self may be shown forth in manifestation."
— Annie Besant, who followed Helena P. Blavatsky as head of the Theosophical Society

"What we need to realize above all else is that God has provided for the most minute needs of our daily life and that if we lack anything it is because we have not used our mind in making the right contact with the supermind and the cosmic ray that automatically flows from it."
— Charles Fillmore in *Prosperity,* a Unity book

"Worldly riches have been feared, despised, condemned, and even hated by spiritual aspirants, because of ignorance of how to be in them and yet not of them, how to possess them and not be possessed by them. Doubtless this attitude of repudiating and ignoring wealth is less deceiving than the other error; greed and the worship of money and the fear of losing riches. But the really wise avoid both attitudes through knowing worldly wealth to be but a reflection of the real, the spiritual riches that must be sought first, last and always. Having found the riches of heaven, you cannot escape the riches of earth unless you purposely repudiate them." — Annie Rix Militz in *Both Riches and Honor,* a Unity book

"Prosperity is the outpicturing of substance in our affairs. Everything in the Universe is for us. Nothing is against us. Life is ever giving of Itself. We must receive, utilize and extend the gift. Success and prosperity are spiritual attributes belonging to all people, but not necessarily used by all people." — Ernest Holmes in *The Science of Mind*

"God is the giver and the gift; man is the receiver. God dwells in man, and this means that the treasure house of infinite riches is within you and all around you. By learning the laws of mind, you can extract from that infinite storehouse

within you everything you need in order to live life gloriously, joyously, and abundantly."
— Joseph Murphy in *Your Infinite Power to Be Rich*

"Refuse to tolerate anything less than harmony. You can have prosperity no matter what your present circumstances may be. Man has dominion over all things when he knows the Law of Being, and obeys it. The Law gives you power to attain prosperity and position without infringing the rights and opportunities of anyone else in the world."
— Emmet Fox in *Alter Your Life*

"Let us learn to think of dollars, as we do of leaves on trees or oranges, as the natural and inevitable result of the law active within. There is truly no need to be concerned even when the trees appear to be bare, as long as we are conscious of the truth that the law is even now operating within to bring forth fruit after its own kind. Regardless of the state of our finances at any given moment, let us not be concerned or worried because we now know that the law acting in, through, and as our consciousness is at work within us, when we are asleep as well as when we are awake, to provide all those added things."

— Joel Goldsmith in *The Infinite Way*

"Remember that money is the consolidation of the loving, living energy of divinity, and that the greater the realization and expression of love, the freer will be the inflow of that which is needed to carry forward the work."

— The Tibetan master Djwhal Khul, through the writings of Alice Bailey in *The Externalization of the Hierarchy*

" . . . it is the fear of the material conditions that wrecks the material body. It is the fear of this or that, that prevents a channel from making for the greater supply." — Edgar Cayce

The Message continues . . . and will continue until it's registered in the consciousness of every soul. The thoughts of lack and limitation *must* be eradicated from the (human) race mind.

The Truth and the Law

1. Your outer world of form and experience is a reflection of your inner world of thoughts and feelings. As above, so below. As within, so without. That is the Law.

2. The greater your awareness of the Presence of God within you, the more that Presence fills your consciousness. That is the Law.

3. The deeper your understanding of Spirit as the Source, Substance, and Activity of your supply, the more permanently that Truth

will be etched in your consciousness. That is the Law.

4. It is your *spiritual consciousness*—your Knowledge of the Presence of God within you as total and complete fulfillment—that interprets itself as every form or experience in your world. That is the Law.

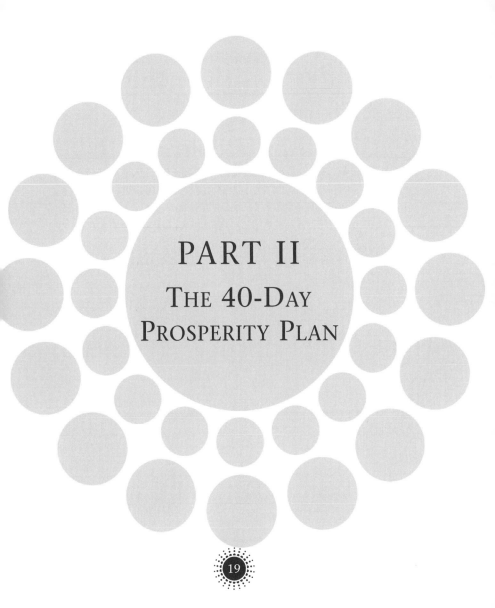

PART II
THE 40-DAY
PROSPERITY PLAN

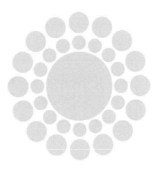

bundance in this book is defined as an all-sufficiency of supply, a full measure of infinite good. In the invisible, it's the creative energy of God, also called Substance. In the visible world, it's that energy made manifest as money and every other good thing required for a free and harmonious life in this third-dimensional world.

There are certain *principles* of abundance, specific fundamentals of Truth, which, when realized, will free an individual from lack and limitation. Since these are *spiritual* precepts, a program for prosperity based on Truth can't be implemented by those with greed, avarice, or selfishness in consciousness. For one thing, a mystical approach used to *get* money will surely fail. However, the same method used to reveal the spiritual cause and effect of abundance will reap rich dividends in both form and experience. Also, since spiritual wealth, both invisible and visible, can only be attained through *realization,* the very fact that the subjective comprehension is held in spiritual consciousness will ensure that the manifestation is for the common good. In essence, the spiritual way to abundance is "rigged" in favor of those with purity of motive. As Ralph Waldo Emerson put it, "The dice of God are always loaded."

Now let's take a closer look at the principles of prosperity—first by examining your consciousness: Do you have an aversion to wealth? Do you object to being rich? Does the word *abundance* bother you? If you have the slightest reservations, then you'd better check your belief system regarding God. You see, God is omnipresent Wealth, the Infinite Riches of the Universe, and the lavish abundance of creation. If you deny unlimited prosperity, you're denying yourself, because *you* are the image of omnipresent wealth, the expression of the infinite riches of the Universe, an individualization of lavish abundance. You're as rich right now as any individual who ever walked the planet. The cattle on a thousand hills are yours, the gold and silver are yours, and an abundance of money is yours now!

The Lord shall open unto thee His good treasure. Your Lord is the Spirit of God, the Christ, within you. You magnify this Master Self that you are in truth by realizing that you and God are one. All that this one Presence and Power of the Universe is, you are—and all that this Infinite Mind has, is yours. Above you, around you, in and through you, is *You* . . . the Reality of You, an omnipotent Force Field embodying all Love, all Wisdom, all Life, all Substance, all ALL. This Allness that's individualized *as* you is the same Mind, Spirit, and Presence who spoke to Moses from the burning bush, the One who spoke through Jesus.

This Spirit within you is forever thinking thoughts of abundance, which is its true nature. Since thoughts of lack or limitation can never be registered or entertained in this Infinite Mind, the Principle or Law of Supply must be one of total and continuous All-Sufficiency. Your Self thinks, sees, and knows only abundance; and the creative energy of this Mind-of-Abundance is eternally flowing, radiating, expressing, and seeking to appear as abundance on the physical plane.

This radiating creative Mind Energy is substance. As this Divine Thought Energy flows through your consciousness and out into the phenomenal world to appear as prosperous experiences and conditions, its "plastic" quality allows it to be impressed by the tone and shape of your dominant beliefs. Therefore, what you see, hear, taste, touch, and smell are *your* beliefs objectified. The form and the experience are but effects—appearances—and we're told not to judge by appearances. To "judge" something means to believe it, to assume that it's true, to conclude that it's factual. But we're told not to do this. Why? Because what appears as an effect has no value in itself—the only attributes that an effect has are the ones *you* give it.

Money is an effect. When you concentrate on the effect, you're forgetting the cause, and when you forget the cause, the effect begins to diminish. When you focus your attention on *getting* money, you're actually shutting off your supply. You must begin this very moment to cease believing that money is your substance, your supply, your support, your security, or your safety. Money isn't—but God is! When you understand and realize this Truth, the supply flows uninterrupted into perfect and abundant manifestation. You must look to God alone as *the* Source, and take your mind completely off the outer effect.

If you look to your job, your employer, your spouse, or your investments as the source of your supply, you're cutting off the real Source. In fact, if you look to any human person, place, or condition for your supply, you're shutting down the flow. If you give power to any mortal as even being the channel for your supply, you're limiting your good.

You must think of money and any other material desire or possession simply as an outer symbol of the inner supply. And the only Reality of that symbol is the substance that underlies the outward manifestation. Money is the symbol of an Idea in Divine Mind. The Idea is an all-sufficiency of supply to meet every need with a Divine surplus in your individual life. As the Divine Idea comes out into manifestation, it appears as the symbol— money. But the money isn't the supply. Rather, it's your consciousness of God *as* your abundance that constitutes your supply. When you try to collect, acquire, and possess the symbol (focusing on the symbol and not the supply within), the outlet for the manifestation closes.

Do you want more money and prosperity in your life? Then shift from a consciousness of effects (materiality) to a consciousness of Cause (spirituality).

When you give power to an effect, you're giving it *your* power. You're actually giving the effect power over you. Does money have power? If you say yes, then you've given it *your* power and you've become the servant. You've reversed the roles.

The Inner Presence—the You of you—is truly the moneymaker. Your thinking, reasoning mind isn't. Your *only* Source is the God Presence within you. If your mind is on the Source, the Cause, then the supply flows freely. If your mind is on the effect, you block the flow. The more *impersonal* you become regarding where your money seems to originate (job, salary, commissions, investments, spouse, and so on), the more *personal* you can become in your relationship with the true Source of your money; and the closer the relationship to your God-Self, the greater the abundance in your life.

Turn within and watch the Inner Presence work. The activity of your Infinite Mind sees and knows only abundance, and in this sea of Knowingness is a spiritual Idea corresponding to every single form, event, circumstance, condition, or experience that you could possibly desire. The creative energy (substance) of these Divine Ideas is forever flowing into perfect manifestation. But remember, if you constantly look to the effect, the visible form, you'll create a mutation, a less-than-perfect manifestation. By keeping your focus on Spirit, however, you'll keep the channel open for the externalization of Spirit according to the Divine idea.

The time must come when you satisfy a need for money by steadfastly depending on the Master Self within—and not on anything in the outer world of form. Until you do so, you'll continue to experience the uncertainties of supply for the rest of your life. Every soul must learn this lesson, and until it does, it will be given opportunity after opportunity in the form of apparent lack and limitation. You may be experiencing such a challenge right at this moment. Realize that this is the opportunity you've been waiting for to demonstrate the Truth of your birthright. Know that this entire experience is but an illusion, an outpicturing of your beliefs, an effect of your consciousness. But you're going to stop giving any power to that illusion or effect. You're going to cease feeding it with negative energy. You're going to withdraw your energy from the outer scene and let it die, or fade back into the nothingness from which it came.

Take your stand this day as a spiritual being, and renounce all claims to humanhood and mortality. Care not what's going on in your world, regardless of your fears about your creditors, your security, your protection, or your future. Turn away from the effects, wave good-bye to external false-belief pictures, and return to the Father's House where you've belonged ever since you left under the spell of materiality. Take your mind off money and material possessions (the effects) and focus and concentrate only on the lavish abundance of Divine substance that is forever flowing from that Master Consciousness within you. Take your stand and prove God now!

Stop adding up your bills; stop counting the money you have or need; and stop looking for your supply from any mortal person, place, or situation. The whole Universe is standing on tiptoe watching you—praying that you'll let go of the negative appearances of the world of illusion and claim your Divine heritage. Now is the time; today is the day. Pass this test and you'll never have to go through it again, but if you yield to mortal pressure and carnal mind temptation to get temporary financial relief from the world of effects, you'll have to go back to the classroom and learn the lesson all over again.

The 40-Day Prosperity Plan

This is a program for realizing abundant prosperity in your life and affairs. It takes 40 days for consciousness to realize a truth. A break during the 40-day period releases the energy being built up around the idea; therefore, there must be a definite commitment to faithfully follow this program each and every day for 40 days. If you miss even one day, start over again and continue until you can go the full period with perfect continuity. Here's the course of action:

- Establish a specific date to start your program, such as the beginning of a particular week. Count out 40 days on your calendar and mark the completion date.

- On the first day of the program, write the following statement in your spiritual journal:

> *This day* [record actual date], *I cease believing in visible money as my supply and my support, and I view the world of effect as it truly is: simply an outpicturing of my former beliefs. I believed in the power of money; therefore,*

I surrendered my God-given power and authority to an objectified belief. I believed in the possibility of lack, thus causing a separation in consciousness from the Source of my supply. I believed in mortal man and carnal conditions, and through this faith, gave man and conditions power over me. I believed in the mortal illusion created by the collective consciousness of error thoughts, and in doing so, I limited the Unlimited. No more! This day I renounce my so-called humanhood and claim my Divine inheritance as a Be-ing of God. This day I acknowledge God and only God as my Substance, my Supply, and my Support.

- There are ten statements of Principle below. Read *one* statement each day. This means that you'll go through the entire list *four times* during the 40-day period.

- After reading the daily statement—either upon arising or before going to bed in the evening—meditate on it for at least 15 minutes, focusing on each idea in the statement with great thoughtfulness and feeling, and letting the ideas fill your consciousness.

- Following each meditation period, write down in your journal the thoughts that come to you. *Be sure to do this daily.*

- Since you've *already* received an all-sufficiency of supply (all that Infinite Mind has is yours now), you can prove this Truth to your deeper mind by sharing your supply on a regular basis while you're working with the Plan. Giving is an esoteric science that never fails to produce results if it's done with love and joy, because the Law will shower you with a pressed-down and multiplied return. But if you tithe (and I really prefer the word *sharing* to *tithing*) as a mechanical and calculated method to please God, unload guilt, meet a sense of obligation, and play a bartering game with the Law, no one benefits—not even the receiver. Give with love, joy, and a sense of fun, and the windows of heaven will be thrown open with a blast!

The Statements of Principle

1. God is lavish, unfailing Abundance, the rich omnipresent substance of the Universe. This all-providing Source of infinite prosperity is individualized *as* me—the Reality of me.

2. I lift up my mind and heart to be aware, to understand, and to know that the

Divine Presence I AM is the Source and Substance of all my good.

3. I am conscious of the Inner Presence *as* my lavish Abundance. I am conscious of the constant activity of this Mind of Infinite Prosperity. Therefore, my consciousness is filled with the Light of Truth.

4. Through my consciousness of my God-Self, the Christ within, as my Source, I draw into my mind and feeling nature the very substance of Spirit. This substance is my supply; thus, my consciousness of the Presence of God within me *is* my supply.

5. Money is not my supply. No person, place, or condition is my supply. My awareness, understanding, and knowledge of the all-providing activity of the Divine Mind within me is my supply. My consciousness of this

Truth is unlimited; therefore, my supply is unlimited.

6. My inner supply instantly and constantly takes on form and experience according to my needs and desires, and as the Principle of Supply in action, it is impossible for me to have any needs or unfulfilled desires.

7. The Divine Consciousness that I am is forever expressing its true nature of Abundance. This is its responsibility, not mine. My only responsibility is to be aware of this Truth. Therefore, I am totally confident in letting go and letting God appear as the abundant all-sufficiency in my life and affairs.

8. My consciousness of the Spirit within me *as* my unlimited Source is the Divine Power to restore the years the locusts have

eaten, to make all things new, to lift me up to the High Road of abundant prosperity. This awareness, understanding, and knowledge *of* Spirit appears as every visible form and experience that I could possibly desire.

9. When I am aware of the God-Self within me *as* my total fulfillment, I am totally fulfilled. I am now aware of this Truth. I have found the secret of life, and I relax in the knowledge that the Activity of Divine Abundance is eternally operating in my life. I simply have to be aware of the flow, the radiation, of that Creative Energy, which is continuously, easily, and effortlessly pouring forth from my Divine Consciousness. I am now aware. I am now in the flow.

10. I keep my mind and thoughts off "this world," and I place my entire focus on

God within as the only Cause of my prosperity. I acknowledge the Inner Presence as the only activity in my financial affairs, as the substance of all things visible. I place my faith in the Principle of Abundance in action within me.

Fruits of the Harvest

Based on letters from members of Quartus, my nonprofit foundation, The 40-Day Prosperity Plan is an effective process in changing consciousness from a vibration of limitation to one of abundance. Here are a few examples from people in various locales:

- "I'm halfway through the 40-day program, and already I'm experiencing daily miracles in my life, and growing marvelously well spiritually. I'm becoming *whole!*"
  — California

- "I'd planned on writing you at the end of my 40-day prosperity treatment. I'm only on day 35, but with the experience of this past weekend—plus the fact that while I'm downtown mailing this letter I'm going to the bank to pay off the note on my house— I feel that it's safe to say that I'm pointed in the right direction. One more note: This most recent demonstration has come almost seven months to the day that I was introduced to Truth, so to those I have run across that seem to be waiting for the far-off day when they receive their enlightenment, today is when it happens, not after x number of books or x number of gurus."
  — Kansas

- "The wondrous results from the 40-day plan have been beautiful." — Ohio

- "I began the program for abundance ten days ago, and the revelations I've been receiving about myself have been absolutely amazing. Today I feel as though I've been given a marvelous shot of cosmic strength and faith, and so I have." — California

- "You've expanded and enriched my pilgrimage in the last year, for which I'm very grateful. I particularly appreciated The 40-Day Prosperity Plan . . . it allowed me to let go of some of the past, and I had an immediate manifestation of prosperity. I'm now ready to move to a new level." — Texas

- ". . . please accept my gratitude for The 40-Day Prosperity Program. . . . I've used it faithfully with excellent results. . . . I notice the increase in abundance already, due, I believe, to the increased and expanded consciousness created by the practices." — Tennessee

- "On the 30th day of The 40-Day Prosperity Plan, my husband was offered a promotion and a sizable increase in salary. On the 40th day, an old bill that we never expected to receive payment on was paid in full. We're so excited that we're going to go through the plan a second time."
  — California

- "I've just completed the 40-day program for prosperity. *It works!* I needed new furnishings for my bedroom . . . what I had was all worn-out, and I didn't know where the money was going to come from to make the changes. Then the day after I completed the program, I received some money, but not enough to buy all that I needed because furniture in my area is so expensive. So I said, 'Dear Lord, this is what I have . . . I'm going out there with it, so direct me to the right place where I can get what I want for what I have.' Well, I found the right furnishings, just as I had visualized, for the right price—with $100 left over . . . and delivered the same day. God is so wonderful! I promise to keep working with the program as a daily prayer." — New York

- "I'm delighted by all the fantastic events that have taken place in my life since following The 40-Day Prosperity Plan. It's a wonderful program, but I must admit that it took me several tries before I reached the 40th day. It's not only a prosperity program, but a program in faith and discipline. I'd get halfway through the affirmations and then I'd be faced with a challenge and quit. My faith was very weak. Yet through determination and perseverance, I've had tremendous results. I'm so thankful to God, because I finally realized what He was trying to tell me." — Missouri

- "I'd been troubled by the thought of letting money rule me. Then I began The 40-Day Prosperity Plan and all things were made new. Thank you!" — Texas

- ". . . I finally did the 40-day abundance program. At about the 20th day, both my husband and I experienced major changes. He now has a wonderful new position, and I've rediscovered my artistic ability to paint. . . . I'm on my third oil painting."
  — California

- "I'm on the fourth go-round with The 40-Day Prosperity Plan, and each time, more abundance appears in my life. I've also noticed that in the process, more junk has been cleaned out of my consciousness than at any other time in my life. Now I know what it means to 'make room for God.'"
  — Texas

- " . . . the 40-day program is showing me the way to live each day in total joy and fulfillment." — Alabama

- "I feel that we're beginning to get a handle on prosperity. During January and February, almost 60 percent of our cash in the bank came from unexpected sources. This is the first time in my life that my employment contributed less than half of my income . . . on Monday, March 19, I will walk into the bank and pay off the loan on my car. Not bad at all, considering I owed almost $5,000 on it on the first of the year." — Texas

Introduction to the CD

The CD that you'll find at the back of this book, *The 40-Day Prosperity Plan* (originally released as an audiocassette), will open your consciousness to the true Cause and Source of abundant living. It's not a program to "make money," although the end result would make it appear to be so. Rather, it's a 40-day activity of mind and heart that *releases* the infinite flow of Divine Love-Supply from within to appear as money, and attract new opportunities for true success. The creative energy radiating as the all-inclusive supply literally interprets itself as everything needed for a life of affluence.

Having an all-sufficiency of visible supply is the natural order of the Universe. We were literally financed by God when we came into this incarnation, and more wealth cannot be given. It's eternally flowing without restriction, yet when we focus on money and other material aspects of the external world, we're concentrating on effects. And to do so removes us from the realm of Cause.

The 40-Day Prosperity Plan takes us back to Cause by conditioning consciousness to be aware, to understand, and to know the truth of our magnificent inheritance. It shows us that to have anything permanent in life, we must *be* it first on the inner plane. When we are *being* rich in mind and our feeling nature, money becomes plentiful in the outer world of effects.

Make a definite commitment to the Plan for 40 days, and follow the instructions carefully. As you find your consciousness expanding, and the fruits of the harvest appearing, add your name to the millions of people who have broken through the web of scarcity into a life more abundant.

PART III
You Are Your Own Money

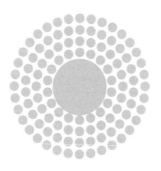

Merriam-Webster's Collegiate Dictionary says that money is a "medium of exchange, a measure of value, or a means of payment." In short, money is what people use to buy things. Nothing evil, unspiritual, or too materialistic there. Money is simply a part of the physical-living process, and in the past it came in forms as varied as stones, beads, feathers, fishhooks, animal skins, and shells.

To establish a standard value in the system, metal coins were later made, each one stamped with a design to guarantee its value. These first were made around 600 B.C. in the country now called

Turkey, and paper money got its start in China during the 1300s. Today we give paper money and coins to people for the things they sell or the work they do.

Simple, isn't it? Where it gets complex is that many people don't have sufficient paper or coins to exchange for the goods and services they need and want. Why not? Because their consciousness isn't attracting, or it's literally repelling, the energy of money. And that's very curious, because the energy of all form, including money, is already an inherent part of each individual's Force Field, an essential part of his/her Light Body.

To help me understand this, I redefined money as follows: "Money is **m**y **o**wn **n**atural **e**nergy **y**ield." Let's analyze each word more fully.

What does *my* mean? It relates to me or myself as a possessor of something. What about *own?* It means "belonging to oneself." And *natural?* It means "God-given, genuine, normal, an essential essence." *Energy?* The word was first coined by Aristotle to express the concept of "vigor of expression." The Mystery School in Alexandria then began using the word to describe "cosmic forces," the Power and Force of Omnipotence, that which we are individualized. Each one of us is the very Energy of the Universe personified. And *yield?* It's defined as harvest, return, payment—in other words, to bring something forth as a result of cultivation or as a return from investment.

With the above understanding, let's now describe money in this way: "Money is my very essence, which when properly expressed, returns to me as an all-sufficiency of legal tender, to be used in exchange for goods and services."

Now we see that in its original form (energy), money has already been distributed equally among all souls on the planet, and an equal opportunity exists right now for every single individual to enjoy a full measure of visible abundance. You are your own money. Money is you!

*Creating a Deeper Understanding of
Money for Individual Prosperity*

In my description of money, three words in the statement need further emphasis. They are: *when properly expressed.* You see, unless you create a *cause* with your natural energy through expression, you can't have an effect. Your energy is expressed (or invested), and the yield is your return in the form of visible supply. How do you express your energy, your very Essence? Through your thoughts, feelings, words, and physical activities all combined in a *daily program* of meditation, controlled visualization, intense love, joyful thanksgiving, verbal harmlessness, and right action—in this case, for the express purpose of cultivating your energy field for the harvest of money.

Uh-oh . . . was there a little blip or negative tug in your consciousness when the term *harvest of money* was used? Do you still think that money is the root of all evil? (The *worship* of money is, but not money itself.) Let me say again that "money" is simply a medium of exchange, what people use to exchange for goods and services, a part of the physical-living process while on Earth, or your energy made visible. Instead of equating money with greed, selfishness, exploitation, and bondage, think of benevolence, generosity, goodwill, and freedom, which are the spiritual values of visible money supply.

Let's continue. We were talking about cultivating your energy field, or conditioning your consciousness. Here's an outline of the daily program I was referring to:

1. *Meditation.* Personally, I feel that The 40-Day Prosperity Plan is a must. Even after the initial 40 days, continue by meditating on one or more of the ten statements each day to maintain the abundance vibration in consciousness.

The principles of abundance as discussed in Part II don't conflict with Part III. For example, I say in the second section, "Money is an effect. When you concentrate on the effect, you're forgetting the cause, and when you forget the cause, the effect begins to diminish. When you focus your attention on *getting* money, you're actually shutting off your supply. You must cease believing that money is your substance, your supply, your support, your security, or your safety. Money isn't—but God is!"

Now look again at my definition of money: **m**y **o**wn **n**atural **e**nergy **y**ield. The *yield* is the effect or the outer symbol of the inner supply, while the cause is your God-given Essence—the Energy that underlies the outer manifestation. Think of it this way: The spiritual definition of *money* is both cause and effect, invisible and visible, consciousness and form, giver and gift. But we don't focus on money-in-form as our supply. Rather, we contemplate and recognize the *energy* of money, which is our spiritual consciousness, and we let the form appear. Please make sure that you understand this point before moving on.

2. *Controlled Visualization.* Before I share the visualization that was given to me by my Higher Self, I want to tell you about a realization I had years ago. In a particular state of consciousness (and corresponding financial hole) that I was in at the time, I kept looking for a miracle. Now miracles are wonderful, and "there's no order of difficulty in miracles"—but the particular miracle that I wanted was the sudden manifestation of money without the consciousness for it. You know, the doorbell rings, and when you open the door there's a huge basket full of money, or the heavens open up and manna-as-money falls in your lap, and so on.

While I considered God as the Source of my supply, I didn't quite understand that Spirit's primary outlet for manifestation in the third-dimensional plane was through *people.* I hadn't had the awakening that each one of us is Spirit's channel for each other. In fact, I turned away from people in a false sense of spiritual pride. *What do they know about spiritual abundance?* I thought. And the hole got deeper.

Until we reach the level of consciousness where we can instantly manifest form out of substance, our visible supply comes through other souls on this planet. Since people are the energy of money, we're in truth sharing ourselves, our essence, with each other.

About this time, someone will raise the point that in The 40-Day Prosperity Plan, I write: " . . . if you look to any human person, place, or condition for your supply, you are shutting down the flow. If you give power to any mortal as even being the channel for your supply, you are limiting your good." And that's a fact! We don't look to any particular individual for our good, nor do we specify any mortal channel as the source of our supply. This is "outlining," and such a practice is in violation of Universal law. However, we do recognize that the "yield" (our visible money supply) will flow to us through and from physical beings living on this planet in exchange for something given. Do you see the difference? Please contemplate this point until you do. Now on to the visualization.

During that particularly tough financial period (or so it seemed at the time), I finally got quiet, went into a meditative state, and spoke these words: "I invite the Spirit of God to think through me. I won't try to think, nor will I struggle to stop my own thinking. I now let the Christ Presence use my mind to think about my financial affairs and the solution to this problem."

Here's the answer that came through: "Know that I am with you always. I am all you seek; seek therefore me. I am the Spirit of the invisible and the visible. I am the Substance behind all things. I am the Energy of Creation. Do as I say do and all will be well. Through meditation, gain the consciousness of the plentifulness of Spirit Substance flowing from the center of your being, which I AM—a constant, bountiful force without end. Embody the infinity of the flow, then release its fullness into the world to prosper all, including yourself. See it as a Light stream connecting you with all souls on Earth. See the Light radiating from you and encircling the globe. The Light stream is now the bridge on which the visible supply will travel to you. After the Light connection is made between you and all the world, see the visible supply returning to you in waves of good . . . rolling, flowing to you from every direction . . . back to the center that you are, that I AM. Let the waves engulf you, then see yourself using the supply in peace, love, and joy. The Light Bridge must be continually supported with and by love; therefore, your thoughts, emotions, words, and actions must be loving at all times."

It was then that I fully realized that we're truly our brother's keeper, but in a different way than I had previously considered. As I meditated on the transmission, the mental pictures for the visualization began to take shape:

. . . the eternal Fountain of All Good within, forever flowing without end . . . the infilling or embodiment of that flow until "my cup runneth over". . . mentally opening the door of my consciousness and releasing the flow to move around this world as a Golden Light, lifting each soul into a new vibration of abundance. I saw the Oneness as every man, woman, and child on the planet was connected in the Light, and I began to see the visible supply being attracted to everyone without exception . . . and I saw joy and gratitude on the faces of people everywhere—a thanksgiving to God—as their needs were met. And then I saw the visible supply begin to flow to me, returning in waves . . . and I watched it coming from all around the world, closer and closer, until, in my imagination, I felt the waves engulf me and almost take my breath away. I felt more prosperous than I

*had felt in my entire life, and I began to
see this money put to work in the most useful, loving, productive, and supportive way.*

In less than 30 days, the so-called financial problem had disappeared entirely. So I ask you to either
practice this same visualization or another one that
evokes a powerful emotional response. A word of
caution: If there's greed and selfishness in your consciousness, the particular meditative visualization
that I described may create great disorder in your
financial affairs. It must be practiced with a consciousness of good-for-all, unconditional love, and
spiritual oneness.

3. *Intense Love.* Ageless Wisdom teaches us that
money is the energy of Divinity, and that in fulfill-
ing our needs, we must work with the energy of
love—not desire. I've found that if I somehow shut
down the Love Vibration, or the feeling of complete unconditional love for everyone, I'm putting

a heavy restriction on my visible supply. And of course, this goes back to part of the transmission I received from within: "The Light Bridge must be supported with and by *love*."

Remember that our "natural energy" is love; therefore, the "yield" is created out of love and returns to us on wings of love. Without the intense radiation of love, there simply cannot be the full and complete manifestation and attraction of supply-in-form.

4. *Joyful Thanksgiving.* Joy and gratitude come from a loving heart. If these qualities are missing in your consciousness, go back to Step 3 and practice the art of loving. Find someone or something you can love (in your mind), focus the love radiation on that image, and then begin to shift it to people and situations that you find difficult to love. Love life and every physical manifestation of life, and as you do, begin to express gratitude for the good that is yours now . . . for the beauty of nature, for friends

and loved ones, for the infinite blessings of God, and for the solution to every problem and the fulfillment of every need. Feel the joy that's rising up in you—that's the vibration that will keep you in tune with all the channels that God has selected for your good.

5. *Verbal Harmlessness.* The Wisdom Teachings also tell us that criticism, verbal abuse, selfish speech, and words of hate darken the soul, poison all life, bring retribution, and remove us from the Way of Wholeness. If you truly want ro maintain your "natural energy" in a positive form-producing vibration and keep your Bridge of Light intact, develop a consciousness that practices only verbal harmlessness. Harmlessness (in both thoughts and words) is the destroyer of all limitation.

6. *Right Action.* If you've carefully followed the first five steps, you'll be led to right action and guided in all your ways. Some examples of right action include: (a) maintaining order in your life

beginning with your body, your home, and your work activity; (b) listening to and following the inner Voice without procrastination and doing that which needs to be done *now;* (c) accepting your responsibilities and doing the best you can in every situation; and (d) acting with grace, poise, ease, and serenity—and sharing your visible supply according to the inspiration and guidance of Spirit—not as a result of outside pleas and pressures.

Regarding the sharing, my wife, Jan, and I proved to ourselves long ago that we simply can't outgive God when it's done in fun, and that the more we lovingly care and the more we joyfully share, the more we happily have. There's nothing devious or manipulative about that; it's just a way of working with the Universal Law of Abundance.

Freeing the (Human) Race Mind from Dominant Beliefs in Lack and Limitation

If enough people would follow these six steps on a sustained basis, we could dramatically change the vibration of humanity's collective consciousness. Perhaps it was best said by Jason Andrews in my interview with him in *The Superbeings:*

> "The good of the whole must begin with the good of the individual . . . you help the world when you help yourself. Remember, we are all one, all waves in the same ocean and one man's consciousness of abundance and well-being with its outer manifestation releases more light into the race consciousness for the benefit of all. So start with yourself."

Start with your "own natural energy" and let it bring forth the "yield"—not only for you, but for your brothers and sisters throughout this world.

ᴡᴡᴡ ᴡᴡᴡ

PART IV

A Prosperity Compilation from Some of My Other Books

From *The Superbeings:*

The abundant life for each individual is the Will of God. God is the source of all prosperity and is forever providing us with whatever we need in abundant measure. (p. 13)

Money itself won't necessarily make a person happy, but a prosperity consciousness will bring forth poise, confidence, contentment, peace, joy, and freedom from the fear of lack—in addition to tangible supply. So money without the consciousness for it isn't our objective. What we want is a spiritual understanding that God is our all-sufficiency of supply in all things. Thus, money becomes a spiritual experience when we work with the principle.

It's interesting that people who have evolved in consciousness to where they can truly be called Superbeings have little concern for demonstrating supply. And the reason is that they recognize that they're the boundless wealth of the Universe in expression. They know that they're related to the One Mind and that this Mind is their inexhaustible Resource. The result? They attract all good things to them in overflowing measure and continually experience the joy of abundant living. They let their minds speak for them, and each consciousness makes its own particular demand on the universal treasury.

How rich can you be? As rich as you think you can be, or as wealthy as your contentment level. However, most people are content in just "getting by," and if that's as far as your consciousness can expand, then so be it. *You* have made that choice. But know that you can achieve the total freedom of financial independence if you choose it and work to uplift your consciousness to accommodate that level of completeness. When Jesus told us to seek the Kingdom, he didn't say to try for a little bit of the Kingdom or half the Kingdom. He said to go for it in its entirety, to incorporate the total spiritual consciousness of plenty in our hearts. And he said to do this *first*—and then all things would be added (attracted) to us.

When we realize the presence of God within us, that realization is the spiritual experience . . . it's the Kingdom of Heaven (Harmony) within you. And out of this Kingdom—this spiritual consciousness—flows everything that we could desire in this life. (pp. 94–95)

A few prosperity secrets:

1. Do not tell anyone (not on the spiritual path) that you are working on prosperity from a spiritual-mental approach. If you do, you will break the connection and drain the power building up in and around your new mental equivalent. Secrecy is an absolute essential.

2. Understand that you are not trying to make anything happen. You are simply releasing

the abundance that is already a part of your True Nature. Eliminate all pressure and intensity. Let the substance flow into visibility and experience. Easy does it!

3. As your good begins to materialize, do not get "puffed up" with spiritual pride. Remember, you are not doing the work. It is spiritual substance that is interpreting itself as the fulfillment of your desires, and you are but a channel for its outpouring.

4. Critical thoughts and feelings of fear will hold back your good, while a consciousness of love and trust will speed up the flow. Love is the fulfillment of the Law, and Faith is the energy that clears the channel.

5. Acknowledge the Spirit within as the one Source of abundance—the one Source of your supply. Look only to God for your prosperity.

6. Do not outline the way your good is to come forth. Let the Spirit surprise you with Its delightful ways of showering you with abundance.

7. Recognize that it is the Will of God for you to be wealthy. Understand that there is not anything that even resembles lack, limitation, or poverty in His Consciousness. You were born to be rich! You are the offspring of the Infinite Abundance of the Universe.

8. Do not delay your demonstration by holding in mind the idea of receiving your good "tomorrow." God works in the *now*. "*Now* is the accepted time." If you live in the future, your prosperity will always be one day ahead of you.

9. Abundance in the physical world is an outpicturing of a prosperity consciousness, so work from within. The higher your consciousness,

the greater your prosperity. As above, so below.

10. Gratitude and thanksgiving are vital ingredients in developing a prosperity consciousness. Nothing opens the door to the Storehouse as quickly as a thankful heart.

11. You develop a prosperity consciousness by changing your mind—by replacing ideas of lack with ideas of abundance. Spend more time each day thinking about what you want rather than what you do not want. You don't want lack, so stop thinking about it.

12. Keep your money circulating. If you hoard it for a rainy day, you may have to spend it on an ark. (pp. 103–104)

From *The Manifestation Process:*

Always remember that your desires are first fulfilled in consciousness, and then they come forth in the outer world clothed with materiality. So the secret is to be thankful while your good is still invisible! You can't wait until you possess the visible form to express your gratitude or you will delay the entire process, or perhaps cancel it out altogether. (p. 30)

If you're out of money, find a way to *earn* some. Do the best you can—even if it means sweeping floors—while you're working on a prosperity consciousness. Remember that God always meets us on the level where we are in consciousness, which means that regardless of where we are in our spiritual development, God can and will meet our needs. But we also have our part to play as a co-creator. And the greater the sense of separation from the Spirit of God within, the greater the activity on the physical plane must be—with each action dedicated to pleasing your God-Self. (pp. 33–34)

From *The Workbook for Self-Mastery:*

When you concentrate on the effects of your world, you're lowering the vibration of your consciousness. The lower the vibration, the more difficult it is for your good to come forth into manifestation. But when you concentrate on the Spirit-Substance of the Great I AM within you, you're raising the vibration of your consciousness. Think on this: While your mind could possibly conceive of a limitation of the form, it certainly couldn't possibly conceive of any limitation in Spirit! (pp. 62–63)

To run around trying to "fix" your world with the consciousness that produced the problem in the first place will only aggravate the situation even more. To change your world, you must change your consciousness. Think of it this way: What you're experiencing in life are your finite ideas projected into materiality. However, behind what you see is what Spirit sees, and that Infinite Vision constitutes the Reality. What about money? In and around and through your financial affairs is the Truth of lavish abundance, the High Vision of all-sufficiency, overflowing supply to meet every need with plenty to spare and share. If you're seeing lack, limitation, and insufficiency, you're looking at the illusion. But as the vibration of your consciousness becomes more spiritual, and you understand that the Spirit within you is appearing as your supply, the shadows of scarcity will dissolve. (pp. 78–79)

Each and every Soul throughout the Universe is a spiritual being—and since my I AM is your I AM, whatever I'm saying about you, I'm saying about me. If I criticize you, I'm criticizing myself. If I see you as poor and weak and unfulfilled, I'm seeing myself as poor and weak and unfulfilled. And what I see or say about myself is conditioning my consciousness accordingly. Because of the way the Law works, if I believe that you're suffering from any kind of lack, I'm calling for an experience of lack in my life. (p. 95)

Your faith vibration attracts that which you have and experience in this world because *like must attract like!* Where is your faith? Look around you. If your faith is in an all-sufficiency, then so it is in your life. If your faith is pulsating to a "just getting by" frequency, then so it is in your world. If your faith is on the dial set of insufficiency, then there will never be enough to meet your needs. Your world simply reflects your faith. (p. 126)

From *Practical Spirituality:*

Your God-Self thinks only thoughts of abundance and never lack or limitation. These thoughts are in the form of pure energy within the Mind of your Higher Self. This thought energy constitutes a momentous force, a power, a mighty thrust that presses out and radiates through your consciousness. This Thought Energy, or Mind Power, is pregnant with the thinkingness of unlimited supply, boundless prosperity, and overflowing abundance. As this copious substance moves through your consciousness, it's either distributed "as is" or altered according to the vibration of your energy field. It lets itself be impressed with the "shape" of your consciousness, and then goes forth into the physical world to become, or appear as, forms and experiences relating to your concept of abundance. (pp. 38–39)

Look at the code words: My consciousness *of* God *as* my supply *is* my supply. Let's break down the statement. First, "My consciousness *of* God." This means your awareness, understanding, and knowledge of the Presence within you—that God Presence, Christ, Spirit, Divine Mind, or whatever term for the Higher Power is most comfortable for you. When you are aware of something, you draw that something into your awareness, which is your consciousness. Awareness leads to Understanding, and understanding leads to Knowledge.

When you turn your mind within and contemplate the Presence, when you focus on that Spirit within, and when you recognize and become aware of the Infinite Mind right where you are, a most dramatic thing happens: At the moment of awareness, you open your consciousness to receive the Presence of God, because the energy, substance, intelligence, power, love, and will of that Presence follows the beam of your awareness! Your entire energy field is filled with the very Spirit of God. Remember, God *is,* but God is *not* in your experience unless there is awareness—recognition of the Presence. Spirit-Mind can express in your world only through your consciousness!

At this stage of your spiritual maturity, Spirit seems to ask you a question: "What would you have me be?" And that's why you must identify the Presence as that which you desire in the outer world. Let's say it's money. Money is a symbol of the Divine Idea of supply. Now let's connect the first two parts of the statement: "My consciousness of God *as* my supply." Your consciousness *of* God *as* your supply fills your consciousness with God as your supply; therefore, your consciousness becomes your supply! We can now complete the statement: "My consciousness *of* God *as* my supply *is* my supply." Can you understand what happens when you embody the truth and meaning of that statement? Your consciousness becomes *cause* to the outer world, and based on cosmic law, "As Within, So Without."

Become conscious of the Presence within as the fulfillment of any desire you have, and your consciousness will outpicture itself as that fulfillment, easily, quickly, and in peace. (pp. 101–103)

A Prosperity Checklist

Ask yourself:

☐ Is my primary interest in realizing the Presence of God, or is it in meeting a financial problem?

☐ Am I still concentrating on the effect (money), or am I focusing my attention on Cause (Spirit)?

☐ Am I willing to take my stand now and prove God once and for all as my all-sufficiency?

☐ Have I devoted the necessary time to meditating on the Spirit within as the Source of my prosperity?

☐ Am I conscious of the inner Presence as my abundance?

☐ Do I have the understanding that my consciousness of the Presence is my supply?

☐ Am I trying to demonstrate money, or develop a greater consciousness of abundance?

☐ Have I accepted the Truth that the living Presence within me is my all-sufficiency, and that the activity of this Infinite Mind is meeting my every need at this moment?

☐ Have I identified myself with my all-sufficient Self so that I can say with great conviction, "I AM Abundance?"

☐ Knowing that my consciousness of the indwelling Presence is my supply, can I now affirm and believe the Truth that I *have* abundance?

☐ Can I see myself fulfilled and enjoying lavish abundance in my life and affairs?

☐ Have I truly expressed a feeling of love for the visions of wholeness and completeness that I see in my visualizations?

☐ Do I intuitively feel that Spirit *has* manifested as my all-sufficiency even though the results may still be invisible? Have I spoken the word that "it is done"?

☐ Have I totally surrendered all my needs, desires, fears, and concerns to the Presence within?

☐ Have I expressed a deep sense of gratitude to the Spirit within *before* my good comes forth into visible manifestation? Is my heart overflowing with thankfulness and joy the majority of my waking hours?

☐ Am I listening to the Voice within for guidance and instructions regarding any action that I am to take in the outer world? Am I following through with that action?

☐ Have I totally forgiven everyone and everything in my consciousness?

☐ Am I practicing unconditional love with everyone in my life?

☐ Have I maintained a state of secrecy regarding the use of spiritual principles in the demonstration of my supply?

☐ Knowing the Reality within all and the Truth about all, can I see everyone on this planet as abundantly supplied with every good thing, regardless of appearances?

☐ Do I desire for everyone else that which I desire for myself?

☐ Am I a joyful giver? Do I freely share my money on a regular basis, knowing that as I give, so shall I receive?

☐ Have I done all that I can do to improve my relationship with my children?

☐ In my personal relationship with my mate or love partner, do I care more about his/her feelings and welfare than I do my own?

☐ Am I working to overcome any problems related to sex in my life?

☐ Am I involved in a meaningful activity for creative self-expression?

☐ Am I working on my Life Plan to see myself as whole and complete in every area of my life?

The more questions you've answered with a yes, the richer you are in mind *and* manifestation. (pp. 120–121)

From *With Wings As Eagles:*

Communication from the Higher Consciousness: "There is a Fountain of Love within you, and from it flows the fulfillment of all you could desire, the light substance to bring every form into visibility. The Fountain is never in disrepair . . . its operation is eternally perfect, and its power source is my love for you, a love so great that it is beyond your comprehension. The flow from the Fountain is endless and bountiful. Will you not stand in the stream with me now and eradicate all appearances of lack in your life? Come to me . . . come within and feel the rushing waters of infinite supply. Indeed your cup runneth over. There is no emptiness in my Universe, no shortages, no limitations. All is forever filled full. Can you understand that I am the Fountain, the Flow, and the Fulfillment? Can you now interpret this as the Source, the Cause, and the Effect?

"Now consider this, for it is very important. There is something between me and your phenomenal world. It is your consciousness. Your world mirrors that which is closest to it; therefore, your world is reflecting *your* consciousness. If you would have your world reflect my nature of loving sufficiency, I must be brought into your consciousness—even to the outer rim, so to speak. There, I stand before your world and the Truth is revealed. No good thing is then withheld from you. But you must not direct or prescribe the way. I am the way. Leave it in my hands. Be as a little child in joyful anticipation, keeping your thoughts on me, caring not and

trusting me, fearing not and loving me. I am the Way!"
(pp. 17–18)

A Thought-Form for Abundance

*I am the Spirit of Infinite Plenty individual-
ized.*

*I am boundless abundance in radiant
expression.*

*What is expressed in love must be returned
in full measure.*

*Therefore, wave after wave of visible money
supply flows to me now.*

*I am a mighty money magnet and oceans
of money engulf me.*

I am wonderfully rich in consciousness.

I am bountifully supplied with money.

I now realize my plan for abundant living.

I see my bank account continually filled with an all-sufficiency to meet every need with a Divine surplus.

I lovingly see myself sharing this bounty for the good of all according to the Father's guidance.

I happily see every bill paid now.

I joyfully see every obligation met now.

With great delight, I see the continuing flow of this money used with love and wisdom as I create the perfect scenes according to my highest vision.

Now create the complete scenario in your mind of exactly how you'll use this continuing supply of money, particularly during the next 12 months. (pp. 43–44)

The Energy of Abundance seeks to express in visible form for the joy of it, and Substance- Light loves to appear and become that which is needed in the phenomenal world. Therefore, the principle of all-sufficiency, including money, is good—very good. And while we won't limit the Unlimited, Spirit won't manifest such an extravagance that it would be a burden. The Holy High Self would never overcompensate by making us *servants* of money. (p. 46)

The Universe doesn't compensate individuals based on the activity of work, but on the activity of consciousness. Accordingly, if you feel your life is empty and useless, that your work is insignificant, or that the things that are yours to do are really meaningless, then you'll be pressing out of universal Substance an income directly related to that consciousness: insignificant, trivial, useless, and valueless. On the other hand, once you see yourself as you are in truth and embody that vision in your feeling nature, you'll move above lack and limitation. You're an heir to all that the Father has, and all you have to do to receive your inheritance is to die to your old ways of thinking. Rising in place will be the Truth of you—a strong, vibrant, useful, significant, valuable, worthwhile, meaningful, loving, and fulfilled individual. (pp. 53–54)

If I dwell on limitation and insufficiency in *any* area of my life, I'm building a consciousness of lack, and lack always attracts more lack. If I say "I can't afford" something, I'm building a "can't afford" consciousness, and the law will bring more things and experiences into my life that I can't afford. In demonstrating an all-sufficiency in my life, I seek the realization that my consciousness of God as my supply *is* my supply. (pp. 65–66)

〜〜〜 〜〜〜

A CLOSING MEDITATION

(from *Practical Spirituality*)

hat do I know of God? God is Life, Life is omnipresent, all is alive. I see this in the wonders of nature, and I see this in myself. I am alive because I am Life. My Life is God's Life, and my Life is God. I feel my livingness within me. I feel God. My awareness of God is growing.

God is Love. I feel Love in my heart and know that this is the very Spirit of God flowing through my feeling nature. I could not love without God. I love; therefore, I am one with God. My understanding of God is growing.

God is Wisdom and Intelligence. God is Mind, and I sense the Infinite Knowingness of that Mind within me. I think and I know, and that with which I think and know is God's Mind in expression. My knowledge of God is growing.

Where is God? God is where I AM, and God is what I AM. I AM an individualization of God and the Spirit of God dwells within me, as me. I AM the Light of the World. I turn within to the Light and say, "Thou art the Christ, the Spirit of the Living God. You are my Spirit, my Soul, my Body. When I look at Thee, I see me." And I listen in the Silence for the acknowledgment from within.

I am now conscious of God, of my Christ Self. I AM the Christ of God, the Truth of God, the Self of God. Through this consciousness of the Reality of me, I open the door to Spirit. I draw into my mind and feeling nature the Wholeness of Spirit and the Allness of God, and my consciousness is filled with the Light of Truth.

I know now that there is nothing that I could truly desire that is not at this very moment standing at the door of my consciousness, ready to appear in my life and affairs. I have only to be conscious of this Truth and every need is met, every problem solved, every question answered. My consciousness of God within is all I will ever need for all eternity.

ABOUT THE AUTHOR

John Randolph Price is an internationally known lecturer, and the best-selling author of 18 books on spiritual metaphysics. He is also the chairman of the Quartus Foundation, a spiritual research organization headquartered in the Texas hill country near San Antonio. He and his wife, Jan, are the originators of "World Healing Day," a global mind-link for peace that began on December 31, 1986, with over 500 million participants. It continues to be an annual event in more than 100 countries.

John is the recipient of national and international awards for humanitarianism, progress toward global peace, and for contributions to a higher degree of positive living throughout the world. He has also received a doctorate degree from the Emerson Institute, and an honorary doctorate in Humane Letters from the Holmes Institute.

For information about workshops conducted by John and Jan Price and their monthly publication, *The Quartus Report,* please contact the Quartus Foundation, P.O. Box 1768, Boerne, TX 78006. Website: **www.quartus.org**

We hope you enjoyed this Hay House book. If you would like to receive a free catalog featuring additional Hay House books and products, or if you would like information about the Hay Foundation, please contact:

Hay House, Inc.
P.O. Box 5100
Carlsbad, CA 92018-5100

(760) 431-7695 or **(800) 654-5126**
(760) 431-6948 (fax) or **(800) 650-5115 (fax)**
www.hayhouse.com

❧❧❧

Published and distributed in Australia by:
Hay House Australia Pty. Ltd. • 18/36 Ralph St.
Alexandria NSW 2015 • *Phone:* 612-9669-4299
Fax: 612-9669-4144 • www.hayhouse.com.au

Published and distributed in the United Kingdom by:
Hay House UK, Ltd. • Unit 62, Canalot Studios
222 Kensal Rd., London W10 5BN • *Phone:* 44-20-8962-1230
Fax: 44-20-8962-1239 • www.hayhouse.co.uk

Published and distributed in the Republic of South Africa by:
Hay House SA (Pty), Ltd., P.O. Box 990, Witkoppen 2068
Phone/Fax: 2711-7012233 • orders@psdprom.co.za

Distributed in Canada by:
Raincoast • 9050 Shaughnessy St., Vancouver, B.C. V6P 6E5
Phone: (604) 323-7100 • *Fax:* (604) 323-2600

❧❧❧

Sign up via the Hay House USA Website to receive the Hay House online newsletter and stay informed about what's going on with your favorite authors. You'll receive bimonthly announcements about: Discounts and Offers, Special Events, Product Highlights, Free Excerpts, Giveaways, and more!
www.hayhouse.com

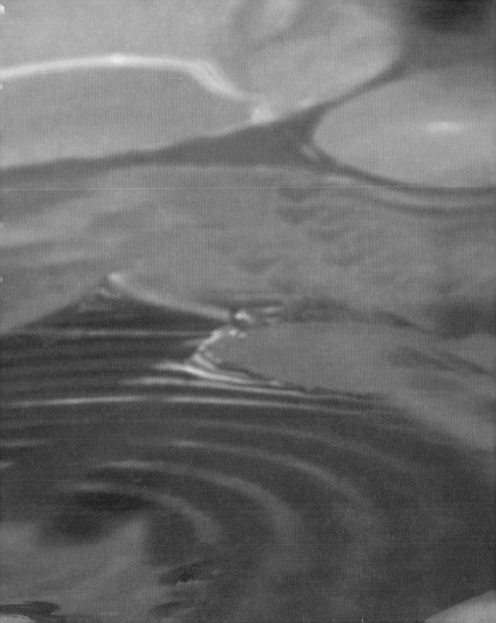

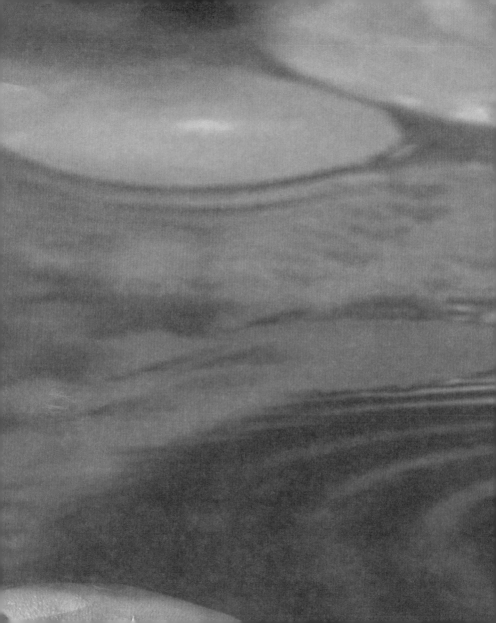